# Anthology 3

T0312370

William Collins' dream of knowledge for all began with the publication of his first book in 1819. A self-educated mill worker, he not only enriched millions of lives, but also founded a flourishing publishing house. Today, staying true to this spirit, Collins books are packed with inspiration, innovation and practical expertise. They place you at the centre of a world of possibility and give you exactly what you need to explore it.

Collins. Freedom to teach.

Published by Collins
An imprint of HarperCollins*Publishers*
The News Building
1 London Bridge Street
London
SE1 9GF

Browse the complete Collins catalogue at
**www.collins.co.uk**

HarperCollins *Publishers*
Macken House, 39/40 Mayor Street Upper,
Dublin 1, D01 C9W8,
Ireland

© HarperCollins*Publishers* Limited 2015

17

ISBN 978-0-00-816046-3

British Library Cataloguing-in-Publication Data
A Catalogue record for this publication is available from the British Library

Publishing Manager: Lizzie Catford
Project Managers: Dawn Booth and Sarah Thomas
Copy editor: Dawn Booth
Cover design and artwork: Amparo Barrera and Lynsey Murray at Davidson Publishing Solutions
Internal design: Davidson Publishing Solutions
Artwork: QBS: pp.11, 12, 13, 14, 15, 29, 30, 35, 36, 59, 60

Printed and bound by Ashford Colour Press Ltd.

**Acknowledgements**
The publishers wish to thank the following for permission to reproduce content. Every effort has been made to trace copyright holders and to obtain their permission for the use of copyright materials. The publishers will gladly receive any information enabling them to rectify any error or omission at the first opportunity.

An extract on pp.5–7 from *Tiger Dead! Tiger Dead!* by Grace Nichols, copyright © Grace Nichols, 2009. Reproduced with permission of Curtis Brown Group Ltd, London on behalf of Grace Nichols; An extract on p.8 from *Gumdrop has a Birthday* by Val Biro, Puffin, 1992, copyright © Val Biro. Reproduced by kind permission of the author's Estate; The poem on p.16 'Bouncing with the Budgie' published in *Star-gazing* reprinted by permission of HarperCollins Publishers Ltd © 2013 Celia Warren; An extract on pp.21–24 from *Greedy Anansi and His Three Cunning Plans* reprinted by permission of HarperCollins Publishers Ltd © 2013 Beverley Birch; Fables on pp.25–28 and pp.29–30 'The Lion and the Mouse' and 'The Ant and the Dove' from *Illustrated Stories from Aesop* , retold by Susanna Davidson, pp.158–163, 169–181, copyright © 2013 Usborne Publishing Ltd. Reproduced by permission of Usborne Publishing, 83–85 Saffron Hill, London EC1N 8RT, UK. www.usborne.com; An extract and illustration on p.31 from *The Dragon's Cold* by John Talbot, pp.5–20, text and illustration © 1986 John Talbot. Reproduced by kind permission of the author John Talbot; An extract on pp.32–33 from *Fabulous Creatures – Are they Real?* reprinted by permission of HarperCollins Publishers Ltd © 2005 Scoular Anderson; Extracts on pp.37 and 39 from *Weird Little Monsters* reprinted by permission of HarperCollins Publishers Ltd © 2007 Nic Bishop; An extract on pp.40–42 from *Let's Go Camping!* reprinted by permission of HarperCollins Publishers Ltd © 2011 Jillian Powell; London Zoo leaflet on pp.44–47, copyright © ZSL, The Zoological Society of London; The poem on p.49 'Greedy Goat' from *Jaws and Claws and Things with Wings* reprinted by permission of HarperCollins Publishers Ltd © 2013 Valerie Bloom. Reproduced by permission of Valerie Bloom through Eddison Pearson Limited; An extract on p.50 from 'Roger the Dog' by Ted Hughes from *Collected Poems for Children* by Ted Hughes and *What is the Truth? A Farmyard Fable for the Young* by Ted Hughes, copyright © Ted Hughes, 1984, Faber & Faber Ltd. Reproduced by permission of Faber & Faber Ltd and HarperCollins Publishers; pp.51–54 reproduced by permission of The Agency (London) Ltd © Michael Bond, 1987. First published by Harper Collins Ltd. All rights reserved and enquiries to The Agency (London) Ltd, 24 Pottery Lane, London W11 4LZ, fax: 0207 727 9037. Three illustrations by R.W. Alley; An extract and two illustrations on pp.55–56 from *The Tale of Peter Rabbit* by Beatrix Potter, pp.31–47, copyright © Frederick Warne & Co., 1902, 2002. Reproduced by permission of Frederick Warne & Co. www.peterrabbit.com; Extracts on pp.57–58 from *The Owl Who Was Afraid of the Dark* by Jill Tomlinson, pp.43–47, and pp.59–60 from *The Hen Who Wouldn't Give Up* by Jill Tomlinson, pp.1–6, copyright © 1967, 1968 The Estate of Jill Tomlinson. Published by Egmont UK Ltd and used with permission; An extract on pp.61–62 from *Kings of the Wild* reprinted by permission of HarperCollins Publishers Ltd © 2007 Jonathan and Angela Scott

Photos: (t) = top; (c) = centre; (b) = bottom

p.18 Shutterstock/John Lumb; p.19 (t) Shutterstock/Ekaterina V. Borisova; (b) Shutterstock/Koshevnky; p.37 Both Nic Bishop (from *Weird Little Monsters*); p.38 (t) Shutterstock/successo images; (m) Shutterstock/Henrik Larsson; (b) cbstockphoto/Alamy; p.39 Nic Bishop (from *Weird Little Monsters*); p.61 © 2007 Jonathan and Angela Scott (from *Kings of the Wild*); p.63 (t) to (b) Gregory Dimijian/Science Photo Library; Shutterstock/Jan-Nor Photography; Shutterstock/Dirk Ercken; Arco Images GmbH/Alamy

# Contents

## From Tiger Dead! Tiger Dead! by Grace Nichols

## Chapter 1

One day Tiger was strolling through the forest and stopping every few moments to admire his stripy face in a stream. Times were hard and suddenly an idea came to Tiger's head that it would be nice to have all the forest all to himself. To himself and his family of course.

The more Tiger thought about it, the more he fell in love with the idea, until he began to speak his feelings aloud: "Imagine me roving freely. Me and my family will have al this to ourselves. No Monkey, Snake, Turtle and the rest to pester me. I must think of a plan to get rid of them, especially that troublesome spider-person who calls himself Anansi. I will play dead to catch the living."

Tiger was so taken up with himself that he didn't see Anansi himself sitting on top of a palm tree, that tricky little spider-man, was the last person Tiger would have wanted to overhear him.

And guess what? Anansi had listened to every single word.

Well, as soon as Tiger got home he told his wife about the plan he had to become king of the jungle.

The plan was simple. He, Tiger, would pretend to be dead and all the animals would be invited to his home. His wife would allow them, one by one, to go into a back room and see the body. As each animal passed by, he, Tiger, would rise up and hit each one down with a big stick. Tiger's children would then drag the bodies away.

Tiger and his wife held on to each other's stripes and laughed until eye-water came to their eyes. What a plan!

Well, bright and early next morning, Mrs Tiger set out blowing a big conch shell through the forest. When everyone had gathered, she burst into tears, telling them about the sudden death of her husband and inviting them to the funeral. As expected, the news was a big shock.

"Tiger dead! Tiger dead!" was the cry everywhere. The news shook the forest. For the rest of the day no one could do anything but talk if the death of Tiger.

"It beats me," said Brother Snake, "it really beats me.

Only yesterday I saw Tiger walking along looking super-strong."

"Must be a heart attack or something," said Sister Turtle.

"Here today, gone tomorrow, eh?"

Only Anansi wasn't present.

## Chapter 2

The next day, all the animals had gathered at the home of Tiger for the funeral. They had something to eat as was custom, and stood around waiting for Mrs Tiger to tell them when to go in and see the body. Tiger, meanwhile, was lying inside, muffling his laughter with a pillow.

Anansi was the last to arrive. He came in style, in his best funeral suit, hat and bow tie. After taking one look at the other crying animals, he drew Mrs Tiger aside and began to talk in a loud voice. Loud enough for both the weeping animals and Tiger inside to hear him.

"Madam," he began, "no one is sorrier than me about Brother Tiger. When I got the news, I myself had to lie down in bed. But are you sure that he's dead?"

"Sure, Anansi!" cried Mrs Tiger. "Who would know better than me who held his hand as he gave his last gasp?" She didn't like Anansi being so nosy.

"Poor Tiger, he was my best friend, you know, Mrs Tiger," went on Anansi, lying through his teeth. "Can I be the first one to go in and see him?"

"I see no reason why not, Anansi," said Mrs Tiger, shortly. It would serve him right to be the first one to get the chop, she thought.

Anansi made sure he had a bite to eat and drink before chatting with the other animals for a while.

Soon it was time to go in and see Tiger's body. Tiger grinned, clutching his stick as he waited. He knew that Anansi would be the first one coming. But as he waited, he suddenly heard Anansi saying loudly, "Oh, I completely forgot to ask, Mrs Tiger. Has Tiger sneezed?"

"Sneezed, Anansi?" asked Mrs Tiger in amazement. "You've come to make fun of a poor widow. Whoever heard of the dead sneezing?"

"Ah, madam," said Anansi, "you have no experience. I have in my travels seen many a tiger die and believe me, no tiger is truly dead until he has sneezed three times. Every good doctor will tell you that. Take comfort, Mrs Tiger. Since your husband hasn't sneezed, he isn't really dead. He will get better."

Mrs Tiger and the other animals listened to Anansi with open mouths. Nobody had heard that one before. Tiger lying under his sheet could not believe his ears, either. If what Anansi said was true, then the animals would think that he wasn't really dead and that would spoil all his plans.

So there and then, Tiger thought to himself, "I'd better sneeze, now."

"Aaahtishoo! Aaahtishoo! Aaahtishoo!"

Tiger gave three loud sneezes.

And that was all it took to send the animals hurrying back to their homes and Anansi laughing, **"Kee-Kee-Kee!"** to the top of his tree.

"Tiger got muscles, but Anansi got brains," was his only comment.

7

## Fiction

# From Gumdrop has a Birthday by Val Biro

**Mr Oldcastle has invited several of his friends to help celebrate Gumdrop's birthday. After they have given Gumdrop his presents …**

The guests gathered round Gumdrop to wish him Many Happy Returns and another fifty years of happy motoring.

"For he's a jolly good fellow," they sang, and "Happy Birthday, dear Gumdrop, happy birthday to you!"

Mr Oldcastle was very happy and he thanked them all for Gumdrop's sake.

"And here is the birthday cake!" he said. But it wasn't on the table – and it hadn't rolled away. It had vanished!

"Who took the cake!" he cried.

Horace was very happy too. He sat on the ground and he looked very fat. There wasn't a crumb to be seen, because he likes cakes.

# Caterpillars

Wiggling, woggling up and down
Painted as bright as a circus clown
Clinging to twigs with tiny feet
Always looking for something to eat.
Some have bristles, some have spots
Some have patches like polka dots
They're brown and yellow, green and blue
But mostly green like the leaves they chew.

**Eric Slater**

**Poetry**

# The Cow

The friendly cow all red and white,
I love with all my heart:
She gives me cream with all her might,
To eat with apple-tart.
She wanders lowing here and there.
And yet she cannot stray,

All in the pleasant open air,
The pleasant light of day:
And blown by all the winds that pass
And wet with all the showers,
She walks among the meadow grass
And eats the meadow flowers.

**Robert Louis Stevenson**

Poetry

# Twas the Night Before Christmas

Twas the night before Christmas, when all through the house
Not a creature was stirring, not even a mouse.
The stockings were hung by the chimney with care,
In hopes that St Nicholas soon would be there.

The children were nestled all snug in their beds,
While visions of sugar-plums danced in their heads.
And mamma in her 'kerchief, and I in my cap,
Had just settled our brains for a long winter's nap.

When out on the lawn there arose such a clatter,
I sprang from the bed to see what was the matter.
Away to the window I flew like a flash,
Tore open the shutters and threw up the sash.

The moon on the breast of the new-fallen snow
Gave a lustre of mid-day to objects below.
When, what to my wondering eyes should appear,
But a miniature sleigh and eight tiny reindeer.

With a little old driver, so lively and quick,
I knew in a moment it must be St Nick.
More rapid than eagles his coursers they came,
And he whistled, and shouted, and called them by name!

"Now, Dasher! now, Dancer! now, Prancer and Vixen!
On, Comet! On, Cupid! On, Donner and Blitzen!
To the top of the porch! to the top of the wall!
Now, dash away! Dash away! Dash away all!"

As dry leaves that before the wild hurricane fly,
When they meet with an obstacle, mount to the sky.
So up to the house-top the coursers they flew,
With sleigh full of Toys, and St Nicholas too.

And then, in a twinkling, I heard on the roof
The prancing and pawing of each little hoof.
As I drew in my head, and was turning around,
Down the chimney St Nicholas came with a bound.

He was dressed all in fur, from his head to his foot,
And his clothes were all tarnished with ashes and soot.
A bundle of Toys he had flung on his back,
And he looked like a peddler, just opening his pack.

13

His eyes – how they twinkled! his dimples how merry!
His cheeks were like roses, his nose like a cherry!
His droll little mouth was drawn up like a bow,
And the beard of his chin was as white as the snow.

The stump of a pipe he held tight in his teeth,
And the smoke it encircled his head like a wreath.
He had a broad face and a little round belly,
That shook when he laughed, like a bowlful of jelly!

He was chubby and plump, a right jolly old elf,
And I laughed when I saw him, in spite of myself!
A wink of his eye and a twist of his head,
Soon gave me to know I had nothing to dread.

He spoke not a word, but went straight to his work,
And filled all the stockings, then turned with a jerk.
And laying his finger aside of his nose,
And giving a nod, up the chimney he rose!

He sprang to his sleigh, to his team gave a whistle,
And away they all flew like the down of a thistle.
But I heard him exclaim, 'ere he drove out of sight,
"Happy Christmas to all, and to all a good-night!"

## Clement C. Moore

# Bouncing with the Budgie

Budgie's bouncing,
Kitten's pouncing,
Dog is fast asleep,
Mum is trusting
Dad with the dusting,
Cooker's going **Beep!**

Budgie's singing,
Telephone's ringing,
Sister's going out.
My room's tidy
And it's Friday
So I want to shout:
Budgie, go on bouncing.
Kitten, give me five!
Dog, wake up and play with me.
Weekend, come alive!

**Celia Warren**

Non-fiction

## Monkey Business

# MORETON *Weekly*

**August 4th, 2014**

## Cheeky Chimps on the Motorway

Drivers were surprised to see monkeys running all over the road yesterday. The lorry taking them to their new home at Burwell Zoo had broken down. While the lorry driver went to get help, one of the monkeys managed to lift the latch on the door. Inspector Baker said the monkeys looked like they were having great fun.

They climbed all over the road signs and scrambled up the lampposts. One even sat on top of the police car! Some drivers got irate because of the traffic jam, but most drivers were prepared to see the funny side. "I'm pleased to say all the cheeky chimps are now safely back in the zoo," said Inspector Baker last night.

# DAILY INFORMER

**August 4th, 2014**

## Komodo Dragon on the Loose

The emergency services were flooded with phone calls yesterday evening, with reports that a large Komodo dragon was on the loose in Newbury, Berkshire. When Tristan Evans, local firefighter arrived at the scene, however, he found that things were not as they seemed.

"At about 6pm we started hearing reports that the Komodo dragon was seen inside a house on Tanner Street. But when we got there, we found out it was just a misunderstanding", he said.

It turned out that the Robertson family had been playing with shadow puppets, one of which was in the shape of a Komodo dragon. This had caused large black shadows in the shape of a Komodo dragon to be seen through the windows of their house.

"We didn't mean to worry people," said Grandma Robertson. "I was just teaching my grandchildren, Emma and Billy, how to use shadow puppets. We were putting on a play called 'Attack of the Komodos'."

Komodo dragons are a large species of lizard from the Indonesian islands. It is recommended that people do not keep them as pets because their saliva is poisonous.

# Thunder and Lightning – a Nigerian folk story

Thunder and Lightning were two grumpy old sheep. Lightning would lose his temper and knock down trees and burn the crops. Thunder, his mother, who had an extremely loud voice, would shout at him.

The villagers became really fed up with them. The villagers kept complaining about the damage – and the noise!

In the end, the village chief said he couldn't stand it any longer. He said they would have to go far away. He sent them to live in the sky!

But things didn't work out as the chief intended. To this day, Lightning still enjoys getting his own back on the villagers, and Thunder still shouts at the top of her voice and keeps the villagers awake at night.

# From Greedy Anansi and His Three Cunning Plans

by Beverley Birch

## Why Anansi the spider has eight long, thin legs

There was once a time when Anansi's legs were not thin and long, the way they are now. They were very think and very short and stubby.

This is the story of how they came to change.

Anansi had short legs, but a large belly, and he loved to fill it with good food. Best of all he liked the tasty food cooked by all his friends in the village.

On this particular day, Anansi went to visit Rabbit. Now Rabbit was cooking fresh, ripe greens. At the thought of the wonderful flavor, Anansi's mouth watered and his stomach gurgled.

"Ah!" he cried. "Delicious greens, I see, Rabbit!"

"My dear friend, come and join me for dinner!" said Rabbit. "It's not quite cooked yet, but it'll be ready soon."

But Anansi was not only greedy, he was also lazy. He thought, "If I stay while the greens cook, surely Rabbit will ask for help and give me all kinds of jobs!"

Quick as a flash, Anansi answered, "Oh, Rabbit, that's very kind of you. Of course I will! I have some little tasks to do and I'll be right back. I'll spin a length of web and tie it round my leg. Then we can tie the other end round your cooking pot. When the meal is ready, pull on my web and I'll rush back."

"Good idea!" said Rabbit. So one end of Anansi's web was looped round the pot, and off Anansi went.

He passed Monkey's house, and there – what luck – a delicious aroma wafted out of the door to Anansi's nose.

"Ah! Monkey," he called. "I smell such delicious beans and honey cooking!"

"Well then, my friend, wait until they're cooked, and share them with me," Monkey replied generously.

But Anansi, of course, feared that Monkey would ask for help.

Hurriedly, he answered, "Monkey, dear friend, that's kind of you! I'd love to share your meal, but first, I must see to a few things. So here's what we can do. I'll spin a length of web and knot one end round my leg, the other round your cooking pot. When the beans and honey are ready, just pull on my web, and I'll rush back."

"How clever!" said Monkey, so one end of Anansi's web was looped round the pot and away the little spider went.

Anansi walked on.

Such tantalizing cooking smells floated around the village!

And there were lots more friends to visit: Tortoise, Hare, Squirrel, Mouse, Fox …

And delight of delights, every one of them was busy making their evening meal.

It's no surprise that for one friend after another he looped a length of web round his leg and the other end round their cooking pot.

Before long, each of Anansi's short stubby legs was attached to the different cooking pots in each friend's home.

Of course, Anansi could only think of the mouth-watering aroma of food that floated around the village, and the scrumptious meals he'd soon be eating.

"I'm really extra clever,' Anansi told himself with satisfaction. "I'll have lovely food to eat and not a single job to do in return." He was day-dreaming happily about dishes of sweet potato and honey, and whose meal he'd taste first, when he felt a sudden tug on the web fastened to one leg.

"That's Rabbit calling me to eat his dish of greens!" In a great hurry, Anansi set off towards Rabbit's house.

But there was another tug, on another leg. "Oh, oh! Monkey's calling me to eat his beans and honey."

A third tug, on a third leg! And another! Then another and another … each of Anansi's eight legs was pulled towards a different friend's house!

In a great panic, Anansi threw himself into the river. In the water he struggled to wash away the webs until his legs were free and he could climb out and recover from the fright.

It wasn't long though, before he saw that his legs were not short and thick and stubby any more. Instead he had eight, long, skinny legs, each stretched and stretched and stretched by the pulling of the webs.

"So that's all I have to show for my clever plan!" he snorted. "Eight spindly legs and eight missed dinners! If I want to eat anything at all today, I'll have to cook it for myself after all!"

# The Lion and the Mouse

– a fable from Aesop retold by Susanna Davidson

The little mouse ran as fast as she could. The bird was after her – she was sure of it. Its wide, dark wings hovered above her in the sky, their shadow blotting out her own on the ground.

Here and there lay little clumps of withered grass, and the mouse darted between them, desperately seeking cover. "It'll swoop at any moment," she thought to herself. "If only I could find a place to hide …" Then, ahead, to her relief, she glimpsed a tree, its snaking roots covering the ground like grasping fingers.

"If I can just make it to the tree," thought the mouse. And she ran on, whiskers twitching, paws scurrying, heart pounding. But just as she reached the edge of the tree, the bird folded back its wings, and dived.

The mouse leaped, paws outstretched and landed on a soft, warm mound. She couldn't help it, she had to look – certain the last thing she'd see would be the bird's sharp beak opening wide. Instead she heard a frightened caw, and the bird shot away, its large wings flapping wildly.

"Hooray!" cried the mouse, dancing up and down. The soft mound seemed to move beneath her, but the mouse didn't stop to wonder why. Instead she scurried on, up and up through what seemed like very strange grass, short and yellow and then long and tangled and then, "Oh!" she cried, bouncing down and landing on something black, wet and cold. The mouse turned around. She was, unmistakably, sitting on a lion's nose.

There was a pause. The lion snored.
"He's asleep!" realised the mouse.
"If I can just …"

AAAATCHOOOO!

As the lion sneezed, his eyes snapped open. He took one look at the startled mouse and roared, "How dare you wake me?" His paw shot out and he snatched up the mouse by her tail.

"I normally wouldn't waste my time eating something as small as you," snarled the lion, "but today I think I'll make an exception." He smacked his lips and the mouse caught a glimpse of a long pink tongue sliding out between terrifying teeth.

"Oh help!" gulped the mouse, feeling sure she was about to be crunched. "Please, please," she begged, putting her paws together and trying to steady her voice as she swayed above the lion's jaw. "Don't eat me. Spare my life today and one day, I promise to save yours."

The lion laughed. He laughed and laughed, rolling on his back and clutching his stomach as if he were about to burst.

"You save me?" he scoffed. "That could never happen. Do you have any idea how small and insignificant you are? I could send you flying with a flick of my claw, squish you with even the slightest pressure from my paw…"

The mouse waited, willing the end to come quickly, but instead, to her astonishment, the lion set her down on the ground.

"Perhaps," he drawled, "I won't eat you after all. You have made me laugh, little mouse. You save me!" He chuckled some more.

"Now go," he ordered, "before I change my mind. And don't you dare wake me from my slumbers again!"

The mouse ran. She scampered all the way home to her hole in the ground without stopping once and when she got there, she stayed there, trembling all the way from her tail to her whiskers.

Days passed. The lion hunted at night and slept in the shade of the tree by day, or walked lazily across the grassy plains, shaking his mane so it stood full and proud. He was King of the Beasts and he knew it. He was scared of nothing and no one. Until … SNAP! He walked straight into a hunter's trap.

It was made of heavy rope and it held him as tight as ten snakes. No matter how he struggled, he couldn't get out. The lion roared in anger and frustration, tears of rage pouring down his golden fur. He knew that when morning came, the hunter would come and claim him as his prize with one shot from his gun. Nothing, he thought, could save him now.

Far away, across that grassy plain, the mouse came out of her hole, her little ears twitching. The sound of the lion's roar reached her and all at once she remembered her promise … save my life today and one day, I'll save yours.

"The lion's in trouble! I must go to him," she told herself. Following the sound of the lion's cries, the mouse ran as if for her own life. She reached him just as dusk was falling, the sky lit like a dying fire by the setting sun. The lion was groaning feebly now, the net close around him like a second skin.

"I've come to help!" said the mouse.

The lion raised his eyes, his expression blank. "What can you do, little mouse? If I can't escape from this trap, no one can help me."

The mouse ignored him and set to work. All night long she nibbled and gnawed at the ropes. She worked fast, scurrying from one spot to the next, never pausing for an instant, even as her body grew weary.

By morning, as the first light filled the sky, the thick ropes of the net had become as thin as the string on a spider's web. The lion stretched and arched his back. One by one, the last pieces of the net snapped.

Stepping forward, the lion shook out his mane and opened his great jaws wide, as if he were about to swallow the sky. "I'm free!" he roared. "I'm free!"

As his voice echoed across the plains, creatures everywhere stopped for a moment and stood still. They knew it for the sound of the king of the beasts. "Listen to how terrible he is!" they whispered to one another.

What have I done? Thought the mouse, filled for a moment with fear. Did I really dare to set the lion free? Surely, he will eat me now.

Once again, the mouse found herself trembling before him. She looked up, saw his great mane bristling, his whole body packed with power, his eyes black as night.

The lion looked down at the quivering mouse. "Thank you," he said. "I see I was wrong. You came to me when I was in trouble. Little friends can be great friends indeed."

He gently held out his paw. "Climb aboard!" he said with a smile. "Together, we can walk across the plains."

So the mouse scurried up the lion's back and watched the sunrise as never before, while all the other animals looked on in wonder, to see a lion who was friends with a mouse.

**Moral:** The strong can depend on the weak.

**Fiction**

# The Ant and the Dove

– a fable from Aesop retold by Susanna Davidson

Ant was thirsty, but the path down to the stream was steep and the stream itself flowed fast and deep. Ant knew he would have to be careful, but he was desperate for a drink.

He crept down the bank, keeping close to the ground, then clambered onto a blade of grass that arched above the water.

"I'll be safe here," he told himself, gripping the grass with his legs. Then along came a sudden gust of wind.

Ant screamed. He tried to hold on but the wind was too strong. He sailed through the air, a little brown dot with flailing legs, until … SPLISH!

The stream carried him this way and that. The burbling water tumbled over him, pushing him down. He bobbed back up again, gasping for breath.

"Help!" cried Ant. "Help!"

He never thought anyone would hear him, his voice a faint whisper drowned out by the rushing water. But then, looking up, he saw a dove circling overhead, as if she were trying to find a way to help. He watched as she flew over to a nearby tree, snapped off a twig from a branch and swooped down to the water. Gently, she dropped the twig in.

With the last of his strength, Ant swam over to the twig and clung on. He was swept past rocks and down waterfalls, until at last he came to rest by the side of the stream. Ant tottered from the twig and kissed the ground, relieved to be on dry land once more.

"Oh that was close!" he muttered. "The water nearly had me there. If it hadn't been for that dove, for that dear, kind dove …"

He looked around, wishing to thank her, only to see a man standing above him on the bank. He had a net in his hand, and the dove was in it.

"Oh no!" thought Ant. "A bird-catcher!"

The dove was fluttering wildly inside the net, beating her wings as she tried to escape, but the man only laughed and gripped the net tighter.

Ant scurried over as fast as he could. "I must get there in time, I must …" he thought.

When he reached the man, he scampered over his shoe and up his leg. Then he bit him, as hard as he could.

Ant heard the man scream and scuttled out again. The man dropped the net and the dove was nowhere to be seen. Quickly, Ant ran on, until he reached an old oak tree. He scurried up its gnarly bark, and there, from an outstretched branch, looked out. In the distance, he could just see the dove, flying free.

"I saved her," thought Ant, with a smile, "just as she saved me."

**Moral:** One good turn deserves another.

## From **The Dragon's Cold** by John Talbot

"Look at this," said Mimi. "Look what I've found!"

"It's very long," said Alex.

"And it's incredibly heavy," said Roland.

"What can it be?" asked Spike.

"It's a dragon!" they all shouted.

"Let's get out of here!"

"Oh, don't go," said the dragon. "I won't hurt you." He sounded very sad.

"What's the matter?" asked Mimi.

"It's this dreadful cold," sniffed the dragon. "It's completely put my fire out. All my family and friends sent me away. 'Duncan' they said, 'no one wants a dragon without fire'."

"We want you," said Mimi, "and we'll take care of you."

"We'll think of something," agreed Alex.

That very night, back in the village, all the sheets mysteriously disappeared from the clotheslines.

Next morning the villagers were very upset. They asked Menzy, the local plumber, to stand watch all night to catch the thieves.

"I'm really wasting my time," muttered Menzy. "I've got so much to do and there's still the town's old boiler to repair. Then, as the moon came out, he saw an amazing sight.

"What are those kids up to?" he thought.

Menzy followed them back to the cave and watched in astonishment. All night long the children sewed the sheets together while the dragon, with his runny nose, slept up on his ledge.

As the sun was rising, Menzy ran back to tell the villagers what he had seen.

"It was huge," he said. "Ooooh, it must have been as long as fifty lengths of pipe. Come and see for ourselves."

From a safe distance they saw an incredible sight – the children had made a huge handkerchief!

Non-fiction

# From Fabulous Creatures – Are They Real?
by Scoular Anderson

## Mermaids and Mermen

Mermaids and mermen are half-human and half-fish. Mermaids often sit on rocks that stick out of the sea. They sing so beautifully that sailors are tempted to sail closer to see them, but then their ships are wrecked on the rocks.

**Are these fabulous creatures real or not?**

**No!** There are legends about mermaids and mermen from all over the world. The god of Mesopotamia had a shaggy beard and a fishy tail. The Roman god Triton blew on a shell to control the weather and the sea.

A long time ago, many sailors claimed to have seen mermaids. Perhaps what they saw was an animal called the dugong which is a bit like a seal. These creatures often sat upright in the sea, holding their babies in their flippers – so, from a distance they could easily look like mermaids!

## Minotaur

A minotaur is a fierce creature that is half-man and half-bull. The place where the minotaur lives was built by a clever inventor called Daedalus. It's a maze of corridors called a labyrinth.

**Is this fabulous creature real or not?**

**No!** The minotaur is an animal from an ancient Greek legend.

In the legend, King Minos sent people down into the labyrinth from time to time. They could never escape from its winding corridor so they were eventually eaten by the minotaur. Then a young man called Theseus went into the labyrinth. He killed the minotaur **and** managed to escape. When he went into the labyrinth he unwound a ball of thread. To get out of the labyrinth, he just followed the thread!

King Minos was so furious about this that he imprisoned Daedalus, the inventor, in his own labyrinth with his son. But Daedalus built some wings and the pair flew away.

## Phoenix

A phoenix is a bird with magnificent gold and purple feathers. When it's about to die, it builds a nest of cinnamon twigs in the tallest palm tree it can find. As soon as it jumps into the nest, the sun heats it so that the nest bursts into flames and the phoenix is turned to ashes.

**Is this fabulous creature real or not?**
**No!** The phoenix is a bird from an ancient Egyptian legend. People believed that the bird lived for a long time – between 500 and 1,000 years. It never ate anything – ever!

In the legend, as soon as the phoenix and its nest had been burnt, a small worm crawled out of the ashes. This eventually turned into another phoenix – so the bird never really died.

The word "phoenix" is Greek, meaning "palm tree" or "purple". In Egypt, the phoenix was known as the Bennu bird.

When someone talks about something "rising like a phoenix from the ashes", they mean it has reborn

## Non-fiction

# Gran's New House

'Seaview'
Cliff Lane,
Sandy Bay,
SY13 7AB


Saturday 6th May 2015


Dear Annie, Tim and Jenny,

We moved into our new house just three days ago. I think we are going to like it, even though it is strange not living in the same town as you anymore. From our front windows we can see the sea, and at the back we have lovely views of the hills.

The removal truck broke down so it took six hours to get here, when it should only have taken about two hours!

Grandad and I thought you might like to come and stay for a few days in the school holiday. If Mum and Dad can't come, then we'll meet you at the station.

With much love,

# Activity Camp Letters

42 Denver Avenue,
Sunny Norton,
SN12 6XD

Monday 18th May 2015

Dear Cameron,

I hope you are having wonderful time!

You've only been away at camp for two days and I miss you like crazy already. I wonder what fun things you have been doing? I hope you aren't feeling homesick at all.

The weather here is miserable. It hasn't stopped raining since Saturday. I suppose at least the garden is getting watered.

Your dad has been working very hard. He painted the bathroom and put up those shelves I have been nagging him about for ages.

Your little brother went for his first full day at nursery school. He clung on to my ankles for a few minutes as I tried to leave but then he was fine and he had a great time. When he came home he had a nap for three hours!

Don't worry about writing back if you are too busy.

Lots of love,

*Mum xxx*

Activity Camp North,
West Yorkshire,
L4 7YK

Wednesday 20th May 2015

Dear Mum,

Thanks for the letter.

I am having the best time ever. On Sunday night we had a
barbeque (there has been no rain here!) and we stayed up really
late singing songs around the bonfire. I haven't been homesick
but some kids have. Tommy Peters cried for a whole hour and he
still isn't totally cheered up.

On Monday we went kayaking in the morning then after lunch
we went abseiling down a massive cliff face. It was about 40
metres from the top down to the bottom. I was so excited that I
volunteered to go first. I felt a bit nervous when I started but
then it was just great.

Yesterday we went for a super long walk up a big hill and down
the other side. I was really glad that I brought those grey
trainers with me that Nan bought - they were very comfy. We were
all puffed out when we got back to the camp centre but guess
what? They had pizzas waiting for us for our tea!

Bye for now.

Love you

Cameron x x x

## From **Weird Little Monsters (I)** by Nic Bishop

## Tarantula

Tarantulas are spider superstars.
While most spiders only live a year
or two, some tarantulas can live until
they're 30 years old. Some are
enormous – the biggest spider in the
world is the Goliath birdeater tarantula,
from French Guiana in South America.
It's as large as a dinner plate and,
as its name suggests, it doesn't
only eat flies!

Tarantulas eat cockroaches, crickets,
frogs, lizards and even mice,
but only a few actually eat birds.
Most tarantulas live in burrows
in the ground. A tarantula comes
out at night, then lies in wait.
If an animal is walking nearby, special
hairs on the tarantula's legs make tiny
vibrations. Then the tarantula pounces
on the animal and bites it, injecting
poisonous **venom** with its **fangs**.

A tarantula will rear up and show
its enormous fangs to scare enemies.
A tarantula's bite can hurt a human,
but only a few tarantulas are
seriously dangerous.

A Goliath birdeater tarantula lies in wait in its burrow.

An Usambara orange tarantula shows its fangs to
frighten predators.

# Ants

## Inside the nest

Tiny tunnels lead into the nest. Each nest is a mass of tunnels and rooms.

## Types of ants

In every nest there are three types of ant. The biggest are the Queen ants. Queen ants have wings. The big males also have wings, but aren't quite as big as a queen, but they do have wings. The small ants are the worker ants, and they don't have wings.

## Who does what?

A queen ant lives in one room of the nest. She stays in her room all the time and lays hundreds of eggs. The big male ants mate with a queen, then die. The worker ants collect the food. They feed the young ants, keep the nest clean, and dig more rooms and tunnels as they are needed. They also keep away ants from other nests.

**Non-fiction**

## From **Weird Little Monsters (2)** by Nic Bishop

### Venus flytrap

This little monster is a plant with an appetite. The Venus flytrap lives in North America. Its large leaves make a sugary liquid that attracts insects – but it's a trap! If a bee or a fly crawls on the leaf, the leaf snaps shut in one-tenth of a second. Next, the leaf oozes chemicals which turn the insect's insides to soup. Then the leaf sucks up the insect soup.

After a week or so, the leaf opens again, ready to trap the next meal. All that's left of the insect are the hard bits such as the wings.

These plants eat insects because they live in swamps where it's hard for them to get all the food they need from the soil. Instead, they get extra food from the animals they eat.

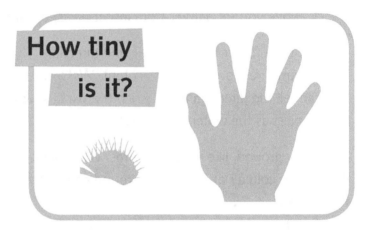

**How tiny is it?**

From **Let's Go Camping** by Jillian Powell

## Setting up camp

When you've chosen your campsite, follow these tips for a comfortable camp.

Choose a level, shady and sheltered site. Don't pitch your tent in the middle of a field where people or animals could pass through.

Trees nearby can provide shade and are useful for hanging out wet clothes, but avoid single trees as they can attract lightning.

Check above you for danger from insect nests, or falling rocks or branches.

**Top Tip:** Do a finger test to check wind direction. This can help to prevent rain or smoke from a campfire blowing into your tent. Wet your finger and hold it up into the wind. You can tell the direction from which the wind is blowing by the side of your finger which feels coolest as the water **evaporates**.

Avoid low ground, like valley bottoms. Warm air rises and cold air sinks so they can hold damp mist, cold air or frost. Low ground can also flood during heavy rain or if rivers burst their banks.

Pitch your tent where it won't damage long grass or wild flowers. Avoid stones, tree roots and ants' nests. Check for animal tracks, especially where animals may be going to find water.

Look to see where the sun is in the sky. Do you want to be in the shade, or wake up to see the sunrise? In a hot climate you may welcome shade, but in a cold climate, you may want the warmth of the sun.

The sun can help to warm a tent if you're camping somewhere cold.

## Tools and skills

**Pitching your tent**
If you're camping, you'll need to learn how to pitch a tent.

**Step-by-step guide**

1.  Unfold and connect the tent poles, then lay them out.

2.  Insert the poles through the outer tent using the sleeves.

3.  Erect and peg out the tent. Pull it taut.

4.  Clip the inner tent to the inside, then peg in the **guy lines** if your tent has them.

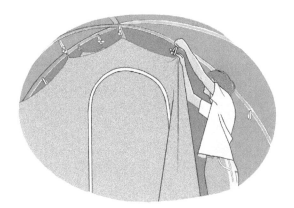

**Top Tip**: Loosen the guy lines at night and when rain is expected, as when rain or morning dew dries the guy lines will shrink and tighten.

## Campfire cooking

There are different ways to cook outdoors. You can use a camping stove or a barbecue. Camping stoves use bottled gas as fuel.

You can heat water and food in a pan or a kettle. A Kelly Kettle is a special type of kettle that you fill with water, which is then heated to boiling point by lighting a fire inside it using twigs inside the double wall of the kettle.

Always store food off the ground away from pests and insects. Use waterproof containers and bags to keep food dry. Dehydrated and **freeze-dried foods** are high-energy foods that can be easily stored and carried. They cook in a pouch or pan when boiling water is added.

# Non-fiction

# On Holiday

**Jo's family is on holiday. They are given instructions and a map at their campsite.**

Welcome to Sandy Bay Holiday Park. We hope you will enjoy your stay with us.

To help you find your feet as quickly as possible, may we offer some advice.

1. Walk around the park to get your bearings.

2. Visit our supermarket to stock up with provisions.

3. Drop in to the information centre to pick up some leaflets about local attractions.

We don't have many rules, but those we do have are to ensure you and other guests enjoy a relaxed holiday, away from the hurly-burly of everyday life!

Rule 1: Please return to the park no later than 11.30 pm.

Rule 2: No noise outside your caravan or tent after midnight.

Rule 3: No loud music at any time.

Rule 4: Swimming pool not to be used by unaccompanied children under 7 years at any time.

Rule 5: No swimming in the pool after 6 pm.

HAVE A GREAT HOLIDAY!

43

# Non-fiction

## London Zoo Leaflet

Le zoo ZSL de Londres héberge plus de 12 000 animaux étonnants. La découverte d'animaux incroyables tout au long de la journée et l'expérience de moments magiques, comme nourrir les animaux ou écouter les commentaires du gardien, feront de cette visite une formidable sortie pour toute la famille. A Pâques 2009 ouvrira notre toute nouvelle attraction pour les plus petits : Animal Adventure, où vos enfants pourront grimper, creuser, s'éclabousser et toucher des animaux dans un environnement unique alliant loisirs et apprentissage de la vie. En visitant le zoo ZSL de Londres, vous contribuerez à sauver des espèces menacées.

ZSLロンドン動物園では、1万2千を超える数の驚くべき動物たちを観ることができます。信じられないような動物の展示が一日中行われています。食事をあげる時間や飼育係のお話をはじめ、さまざまな動物たちの神秘的な瞬間を目撃することができ、誰にとっても素晴らしい一日を過ごせる場所です。また、2009年イースターには、最新の子供用アトラクションが公開されます。これはアニマル・アドベンチャーと呼ばれ、丘を登ったり、トンネルをくぐったり、水に踏み込んだりしながら動物たちと遊べる特別の空間で、活きいきと楽しみながら学べる場所です。そしてZSLロンドン動物園に遊びにくるだけで、絶滅の危機にある動物たちを救う手助けもできるのです。

Lo Zoo di Londra, gestito dalla Zoological Society of London (ZSL), ospita più di 12.000 fantastici animali tutti da vedere. Grazie alle sorprendenti specie in mostra durante tutto il giorno e alla magia di numerosi momenti unici, tra cui assistere al pasto degli animali e alle dimostrazioni dei custodi, la visita al giardino zoologico è una gita fantastica per tutta la famiglia. A Pasqua 2009 aprirà una nuovissima attrazione per i ragazzi, l'Animal Adventure, che permetterà di arrampicarsi, percorrere tunnel, schizzare acqua e toccare gli animali in un ambiente speciale, dove apprendere divertendosi. Visitando lo Zoo di Londra darete il vostro contributo alla salvaguardia delle specie a rischio d'estinzione.

El Zoo de Londres tiene más de 12.000 animales asombrosos que ver. Cuenta con exposiciones increíbles sobre animales durante todo el día y se pueden ver muchos momentos mágicos con los animales, como cuando les dan de comer o hay charlas de los cuidadores. Visitar el Zoo de Londres supone pasar un gran día para todos. En Semana Santa de 2009 presentaremos nuestra nueva atracción para niños: "Animal Adventure" (Aventura Animal), en la que podrán escalar, pasar por túneles, salpicar y tocar a los animales, y todo dentro de un entorno especial divertido y en el que aprender sobre la vida real. Al visitar el Zoo de Londres ayudará a proteger las especies en peligro.

Зоологическое общество «Лондонский зоопарк» предлагает Вам возможность увидеть более 12000 видов удивительных животных. На протяжении всего дня можно наблюдать за удивительными животными, включая «особые» времена кормления зверей и рассказы смотрителей зоопарка. Все это сделает пребывание в зоопарке незабываемым для посетителей всех возрастов и интересов. Начиная с пасхальных каникул 2009 года, мы открываем новый аттракцион для детей «Приключение в мире животных», где можно полазить и вверх и по тоннелям, поплескаться в воде и потрогать животных в особой обстановке, что будет увлекательно и поучительно, позволит приобрести, важные для жизни знания. Посещая Лондонский зоопарк, Вы помогаете сохранять исчезающие виды животных.

Im ZSL London Zoo gibt es über 12.000 spannende Tiere zu beobachten. Mit seinen faszinierenden Tierausstellungen während des gesamten Tages und zahlreichen verzaubernden Tiermomenten einschließlich Fütterungen und Tierpfleger-Aktionen, ist der Zoo für alle ein tolles Ausflugsziel. Zu Ostern 2009 wird unsere brandneue Attraktion für Kinder eröffnet: Animal Adventure. Hier können die Kleinen in einer außergewöhnlichen Naturumgebung klettern, durch Tunnel laufen und Tiere nass spritzen oder auch streicheln, sodass ihnen mit viel Spaß tolle Erfahrungen sammeln. Durch einen Besuch beim ZSL London Zoo tragen Sie aktiv zum Schutz gefährdeter Tierarten bei.

倫敦ZSL 動物園有逾 12,000 頭神奇的動物供您觀賞。憑藉匪夷所思的全天動物展出和諸多的神奇動物時刻(包括動物餵食和同養員交淡),這是老少皆宜的出游活動。我們為孩子們準備的全新節目：Animal Adventure(動物探險之旅)將於 2009 年復活節開始；其中，孩子們可以攀爬、鑽洞、涉水，以及在充滿樂趣和知識的特殊環境中觸摸動物。透過造訪 ZSL 倫敦動物園，您將為拯救瀕危物種盡一份力。

# How t

**Open every day from 10am**

Closing times vary, pl
see zsl.org for deta
Closed Christmas D

**By tube & bus**

**Camden Town** (Northern
10 min walk - follow sign
ZSL London Zoo or catch
274 bus towards Baker St
(5 min bus).

**Regent's Park** (Bakerloo L
20 min walk - follow signs
through Regent's Park.

**Baker Street** (Bakerloo Li
15 min bus - Catch a 274
towards Camden Town.

This leaflet is available
Please contact us if

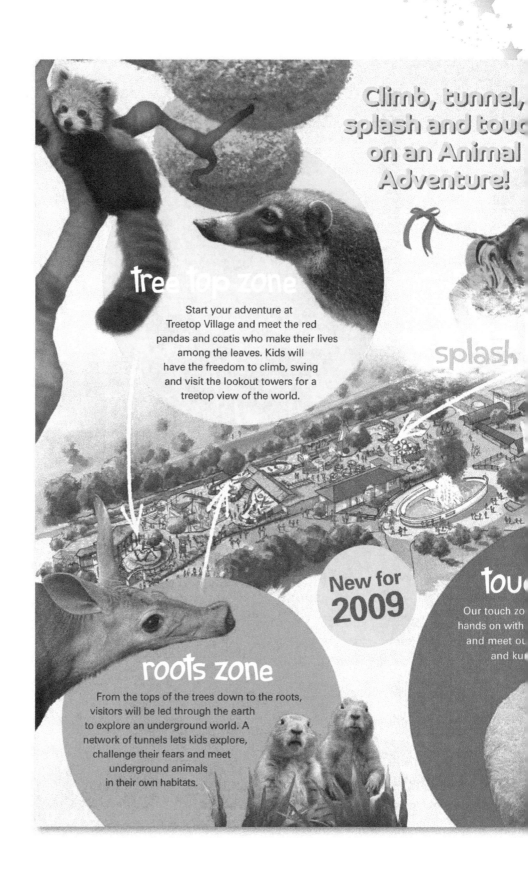

Climb, tunnel,
splash and touc
on an Animal
Adventure!

### tree top zone

Start your adventure at
Treetop Village and meet the red
pandas and coatis who make their lives
among the leaves. Kids will
have the freedom to climb, swing
and visit the lookout towers for a
treetop view of the world.

splash

New for
2009

touc

Our touch zo
hands on with
and meet ou
and ku

### roots zone

From the tops of the trees down to the roots,
visitors will be led through the earth
to explore an underground world. A
network of tunnels lets kids explore,
challenge their fears and meet
underground animals
in their own habitats.

**nimal venture**

Our water based zone near the shop and café lets children play and learn how water gives life and the importance of conserving the environment. This area allows you to become active in our mini stream, take a seat in our secret garden or be enchanted by some story telling in the tipi.

**le**

get goats nas

Visit Africa in the heart of London. Experience the sights, sounds and smells of the rainforest and get closer than ever to our gorillas.

**GORILLA KINGDOM**

**Clore Rainforest**

**BLACKBURN PAVILION**

Come face to face with an amazing array of exotic birds including the only hummingbirds on view in the UK.

**INTO AFRICA**

**Meet The Monkeys**

**DON'T MISS**

Giant Galapagos Tortoises coming soon

**ZSL** LIVING CONSERVATION

The Zoological Society of London (ZSL) is a charity devoted to the worldwide conservation of animals and their habitats through breeding endangered species at ZSL London Zoo and ZSL Whipsnade Zoo; carrying out research in conservation biology and managing conservation programmes in over 30 countries worldwide, including the United Kingdom. For more information visit zsl.org Registered charity in England and Wales: no 208728.

ZSL is committed to limiting its impact on the natural environment. This leaflet is made from at least 75% recycled paper and uses vegetable based inks from sustainable raw materials.

# Fun on Bikes

# ANNUAL YOUNG BIKERS' CHAMPIONSHIP

**Crossfield Farm, Westergate**
**Saturday 25th October**

*Juniors (7–10 years) 10.00-12.30*
*Senior (11–14 years) 12.30-3.00*

*(Sorry – no under-7 bikers allowed to enter)*

**Entrance fees:**
**Riders free    Spectators £1.00**

**Refreshment tent**

48

# Poetry
## Greedy Goat

My goat eats anything,
Paper, cardboard, bits of string,
Apple pips or orange peel,
To goat it's just another meal.

Goat eats baskets, nibbles clothes,
Dolls and teddies, she'll eat those.
She took my pyjamas the other day,
I yelled, but she ate them anyway.

Aunt Rebecca's brand new hat,
Greedy goat said, "I'll have that!"
But even goat won't eat broccoli,
So why are you feeding it to me?

**Valerie Bloom**

## Poetry
# Roger the Dog

Asleep he wheezes at his ease.
He only wakes to scratch his fleas.

He hogs the fire, he bakes his head
As if he were a loaf of bread.

He's just a sack of snoring dog.
You lug him like a log.

You can roll him with your foot,
He'll stay snoring where he's put.

I take him out for exercise,
He rolls in cowclap up to his eyes.

He will not race, he will not romp,
He saves his strength for gobble and chomp.

He'll work as hard as you could wish
Emptying his dinner dish,

Then flops flat, and dips down deep,
Like a miner, into sleep.

**Ted Hughes**

# Paddington and the Marmalade Maze

by Michael Bond

One day, Paddington's friend, Mr Gruber, took him on an outing to a place called Hampton Court Palace.

"I think you will enjoy it, Mr Brown," he said as they drew near. "It's very old and it has over one thousand rooms. Lots of Kings and Queens have lived here."

Paddington always enjoyed his outings with Mr Gruber and he couldn't wait to see inside the Palace.

As they made their way through an arch, Mr Gruber pointed to a large clock. "That's a very special clock," he said. "It not only shows the time, it tells you what month it is."

"Perhaps we should hurry, Mr Gruber," said Paddington anxiously. "It's half past June already."

They hadn't been inside the Palace very long before they came across a room which had the biggest bed Paddington had ever seen.

"Queen Anne used to sleep in it," said Mr Gruber.

"I expect they put the rope round it to stop her falling out when she had visitors," said Paddington, looking at all the people.

"This is known as the 'Haunted Gallery'," said Mr Gruber. "They do say that when Catherine Howard's ghost passes by you can feel a cold draught."

Paddington shivered. "I hope she's got a duffle coat like mine!" he said.

Mr Gruber took Paddington to see the kitchen next.

"In the old days they used to have wood fires," he explained. "That's why there is such a high ceiling. There was a lot of smoke."

"I was hoping they might have left some Royal buns behind," said Paddington, licking his lips.

"Talking of buns," said Mr Gruber, "I think it's time we had our lunch."

He led the way outside and they sat down together on the edge of a pool. As Paddington opened his suitcase he accidentally dropped one of his sandwiches into the water. It was soon alive with goldfish.

"They must like marmalade," said Mr Gruber. "I wonder if that's how they got their name?"

When they had finished their sandwiches, Mr Gruber took Paddington to see 'The Great Vine'.

"It's very famous," he said. "Every year they pick over five hundred bunches of grapes. Imagine that, Mr Brown!"

"I'm trying to, Mr Gruber," said Paddington. "I think I might plant a grape pip when I get back home."

52

Mr Gruber chuckled. "I'm afraid you will have a long wait, Mr Brown," he said. "That vine is over two hundred years old."

"Now," said Mr Gruber, "before we leave we must visit the famous maze. Sometimes it takes people hours to find their way out."

"I hope that doesn't happen to us," said Paddington. "My paws are getting tired."

"Perhaps it's time I took you home," said Mr Gruber.

Much to his surprise, the words were no sooner out of his mouth than everyone around them began to talk.

"Hey, that sounds a great idea," said a man in a striped shirt.

"Please to wait while I buy a new film for my camera," said a Japanese lady.

"I've never been inside a real English home before," said another lady. "I wonder if they serve tea?"

"Oh, dear!" whispered Mr Gruber. "They must think I'm one of the guides. What shall we do?"

"Mrs Bird won't be very pleased if they all follow us home," exclaimed Paddington. "She only has a small teapot."

Then he had an idea.

"Follow me," he called. "I think perhaps we ought to go in the maze after all."

"Are you sure we are doing the right thing?" gasped Mr Gruber, as he hurried on behind.

"Bears are good at mazes," said Paddington. "You need to be in darkest Peru. The forests are very thick."

And sure enough, before Mr Gruber had time to say any more, Paddington had led the way out, leaving everyone else inside.

"How ever did you manage to do that, Mr Brown?" gasped Mr Gruber.

"Quickest visit I've ever seen," agreed the man in the ticket office.

"I used marmalade chunks to show where we had been," said Paddington. "It's something my Aunt Lucy taught me before she went into the Home for Retired Bears."

"But I thought you had eaten all your sandwiches," said Mr Gruber.

"I always keep a spare one under my hat in case I have an emergency," said Paddington.

"That's something else Aunt Lucy taught me. She'll be very pleased when she hears."

And he stopped at a kiosk to buy a picture postcard so that he could write and tell her all about his day out.

That night when he went to bed, as well as the postcard and a pen, Paddington took some rope.

"It's something Queen Anne used to do," he announced. "I've a lot to tell Aunt Lucy and I don't want to fall out of bed before I've finished."

# From **The Tale of Peter Rabbit** by Beatrix Potter

**Peter lived with his family in a sand-bank, under the roots of a big fir tree. He was always a problem for his mother, causing trouble and getting into scrapes.**

"Now, my dears," said old Mrs. Rabbit one morning, "you may go into the fields or down the lane, but don't go into Mr. McGregor's garden. Your Father had an accident there; he was put into a pie by Mrs. McGregor. Now run along and don't get into mischief. I am going out."

Flopsy, Mopsy and Cotton-tail went down the lane to gather blackberries; But Peter, who was very naughty, ran straight away to Mr. McGregor's garden and squeezed under the gate!

First he ate some lettuces and some French beans; and then
he ate some radishes; and then, feeling rather sick,
he went to look for some parsley. But round the
end of the cucumber frame, who should he
meet but Mr. McGregor!

Mr. McGregor was on his hands and knees
planting out cabbages, but he jumped
up and ran after Peter, waving a rake
and calling out, "Stop thief!"

Peter was most dreadfully frightened;
he rushed all over the garden, for he had
forgotten the way back to the gate.
He lost one of his shoes among the
cabbages, and the other shoe
amongst the potatoes.

After losing them, he ran on four legs and went faster, so that I think he might have got
away altogether if he had not unfortunately run into a gooseberry net, and got caught
on the large buttons on his jacket. It was a blue jacket with brass buttons, quite new.

Peter gave himself up for lost, and shed big tears; but his sobs were overheard by
some friendly sparrows, who flew to him in great excitement, and implored him to
exert himself.

Mr. McGregor came up with a sieve, which he intended to pop upon the top of Peter;
but Peter wriggled out just in time, leaving his jacket behind him, and rushed into the
tool shed, and jumped into a can. It would have been a beautiful thing to hide in, if it
had not had so much water in it.

Mr. McGregor was quite sure that Peter was somewhere in the tool-shed, perhaps hidden
underneath a flower-pot. He began to turn them over carefully, looking under each.

Presently Peter sneezed – "Kertyschoo!" Mr. McGregor was after him in no time,
and tried to put his foot upon Peter, who jumped out of a window, upsetting three
plants. The window was too small for Mr. McGregor, and he was tired of running after
Peter. He went back to his work.

Peter sat down to rest; he was out of breath and trembling with fright, and he had not
the least idea which way to go. Also he was very damp with sitting in that can.

# From **The Owl Who Was Afraid of the Dark**

by Jill Tomlinson

**Mother Owl was getting fed up with Plop, a young owl who was afraid of the dark.**

'Go and find out some more about the dark, please, dear.' .

Now?' said Plop.

'Now,' said his mother. 'Go and ask that little girl what she thinks about it.'

'What little girl?'

'That little girl sitting down there – the one with the pony-tail.'

'Little girls don't have **tails**.'

'This one does. Go now or you'll miss her.'

So Plop shut his eyes, took a deep breath, and fell off his branch. His landing was a little better than usual. He bounced three times and rolled gently towards the little girl's feet.

'Oh, a woolly ball!' cried the little girl.

'Actually, I'm a barn owl,' said the woolly ball.

'An owl? Are you sure?' she said, putting out a grubby finger and prodding Plop's round fluffy tummy.

'Quite sure,' said Plop, backing away and drawing himself up tall.

'Well, there's no need to be huffy,' said the little girl. 'You bounced. You must expect to be mistaken for a ball if you go bouncing about the place. I've never met an owl before. Do you say 'Tu-wit-a-woo'?'

'No,' said Plop, 'That's Tawny Owls.'

'Oh, you can't be a proper owl then,' said the little girl. '**Proper** owls say 'Tu-whit-a-woo'!'

'I **am** a proper owl!' said Plop, getting very cross. 'I am a barn owl, and barn owls go 'Eeeek' like that.

'Oh, don't **do** that!' said the little girl, putting her hands over her ears.

'Well, you shouldn't have made me cross,' said Plop. 'Anyway – **you** can't be a proper girl. '

'**W'hat** did you say?' said the little girl, taking her hands off her ears.

'I said you're not a proper girl. Girls don't have tails. Squirrels have tails, rabbits have tails, mice …'

'This is a pony-tail,' said the little girl. 'It's the longest one in the class,' she added proudly.

'But why do you want to look like a pony?' asked Plop.

'Because – oh, because it's the fashion,' said the little girl. 'Don't you know **anything**?'

'Not much,' agreed Plop. 'Mummy says that that is why I'm afraid of the dark – because I don't know anything about it. Do **you** like the dark?'

The little girl looked at Plop in surprise. 'Well, of course I do,' she said. 'There has to be dark. DARK IS NECESSARY.'

'Dark is nessessess – is whatter?'

'Necessary. We need it. We can't do without it.' 'I could do without it,' said Plop. 'I could do without it very nicely.'

# From **The Hen Who Wouldn't Give Up** by Jill Tomlinson

### Hilda has an upsetting morning

Hilda was a hen – a small, brown, speckled hen –
and she lived on Biddick's Farm in a village called
Little Dollop.

Hilda was very excited. Her auntie had just hatched
out five baby chicks. Hilda was dying to see them.
The trouble was, her auntie lived in Much Wallop,
and that was five miles away. How was Hilda going
to get there? It was too far to walk.

She sat in her favourite spot under the hedge and
had a good think.

Suddenly Hilda perked up her head. Of course!
She would have to get a lift.

She squeezed through the hedge and hurried down
the muddy lane from the farm.

There'll be lots of cars and things on the main road, she said to herself. I'll be in Much
Wallop in no time. Won't Auntie be surprised to see me!

But when Hilda reached the road there was nothing in sight.

Perhaps I shall find something further on, she thought, and set off in the direction of
Much Wallop.

She was in luck. Just around the corner there was a row of cottages, and parked in front
of them was a big, green, lorry thing.

It was rather an odd box-like shape, with an open
half-door at the back. Hilda hopped on to this and
peered inside. She could not see very clearly, but it
seemed to be full of torn packets and ashes and old
tins. It smelled very nasty.

Still, this was no time to be fussy. Hilda hopped
daintily down and settled on an old cornflake packet.

There were a few cornflakes left in it. Hilda was very
fond of cornflakes.

She was just finishing the last one when she had a terrible shock. There was a great clanging and banging, and then a shower of horrible things was poured on top of her! She was battered and bumped by rotten apples and sticky baked-bean tins and spiky fish bones and – ugh! – all sorts of unspeakable things. Hilda was too shocked to squawk.

She thought she was going to be buried alive.

At last it stopped, but worse was to come. A voice shouted, 'All right, Bill! Up she goes!' and the whole thing begins to tip up.

This helped at first, because all the rubbish rolled off Hilda again and unburied her, but it went on tipping until all the rubbish was piled at the other end of the cart, with Hilda, fluttering and furious, tumbled on top of it. It was bad enough to have dustbins emptied on her head, but to be turned upside-down as well! It was too much.

Hilda spread her wings and fluttered to the open end of the cart, which was now facing up to the sky.
Just as she got there, the whole thing began to swing down again. Hilda clung desperately to the tailboard as it plunged to earth. When it stopped, she hopped down and began to run. She did not stop running until she was safely back in the farm lane again. She was shaking all over.

'Oh dear,' she clucked, collapsing into a sad little heap by the ditch. 'Oh dear, dear!'

When she had rested a little, Hilda shook the dust out of her feathers and had a good wash in the ditch.

She felt a lot better after that.

'Silly me!' she muttered to herself as she pecked away at a patch of treacle on her tail. 'I **would** choose a rubbish cart! Never mind. I'm going to see Auntie's chicks somehow. I'll try again tomorrow – on something cleaner!'

And brave little Hilda cocked her head and set off home to the farm.

From **Kings of the Wild** by Jonathan and Angela Scott

## Brown bear country

Welcome to brown bear country. Brown bears are some of the largest meat-eating animals on Earth, and carve out a life in the rocky shorelines, mountains and forests in the most northern countries of the globe. In these conditions brown bears have to be tough, strong animals to survive.

### What do brown bears look like?

Brown bears can be all different colours of brown from almost cream or golden to darkest chocolate. Their fur can sometimes look frosted with tips of white or tan and in North America, if they are living inland, they are often called grizzly bears.

Whatever their colour, you can spot them because their large, well-developed shoulder muscles form a hump on their shoulders and their faces aren't as round as those of black bears.

Polar bears are the largest bears, but brown bears are also very large. A male brown bear can stand over three metres high and weigh 600 kilograms or more. That's as much as six or seven grown men. Female bears are smaller than male bears. The biggest brown bears live along the coast in Alaska.

Brown bears often stand upright on two legs. Sometimes it's because they're curious and want to see what's going on, and sometimes it's because they want to reach higher up a tree for food. They also do this to threaten other animals.

Brown bears are very powerful animals. They can climb and swim and they are especially good at digging holes. But in spite of their size, they can also run fast – they can chase and catch a deer running at 50 kilometres per hour

Bears can't draw in their front claws, which are often as much as 12 centimetres long. Their back claws are only half that length. They often use their great forepaws like hands to feed themselves.

Bears can sniff out food from far away, even when it's locked inside cars. They also have very good hearing and eyesight. Bears can see in colour unlike dogs, which are related to them. This is probably to help them know which berries and shoots are good to eat.

**Where do brown bears live?**

Brown bears live in some of the wildest places on Earth. They've learnt to survive in forest areas where they can easily hide, river valleys where there's plenty of food, grassy meadows and on remote coasts. They also live on the cold northern plains south of the Arctic circle. A few bears still remain in the mountains of Europe and Asia, but today they mostly live in Canada, Alaska or Russia.

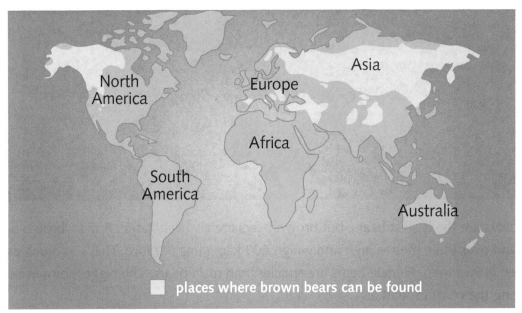

places where brown bears can be found

# Funny Feeders

### Fast feeders

Many **frogs** have long tongues. They can shoot them out extremely quickly to catch their food, usually an insect. Then they bring their tongue – and the insect – back into their mouth.

### Watching and waiting

**Vultures** don't kill animals. They circle around waiting for an animal to die, or be killed. Then they swoop down to feed.

### Killer plants

Many insects eat plants, but **Venus flytraps** are plants that attack insects! They can close up their leaves to trap an insect. When the insect dies, the Venus flytrap can digest and feed on it.

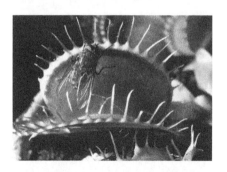

### Plant parasites

Some plants live off other plants. They feed off the other plants without killing it. We call them parasites. **Mistletoe**, which grows in the branches of a tree, is a parasite.

**Mosquitoes** and some other small creatures, like **fleas**, are also parasites. They live on other animals (including people, sometimes!). They make tiny holes through the skin and suck the blood.